To Mom...Your inner resources и

I miss you every day. Love, Jackie

Dear EMDR Therapist,

Welcome to Play Therapy Community's ™ Animal Imagery Inner Resource Development book! The images in this book provide visual representation of a variety of potential inner resources.

Below are some directive ideas. However, I encourage you go beyond these directives when appropriate. Also, incorporate the identified resources in subsequent work when relevant to best support your clients.

- Which animals have positive characteristics that you have as well? (compassion, love, empathy, confidence, strength, etc.)

- Which animals are nurturers?

- Which animals are protectors?

Take care,
Jackie Flynn

Certified EMDR Therapist
Registered Play Therapist

41

67474875R00024

Made in the USA
San Bernardino, CA
23 January 2018